THE STORY OF THE
BOSTON CELTICS

THE NBA:
A HISTORY
OF HOOPS

THE STORY OF THE
BOSTON
CELTICS

JIM WHITING

CREATIVE EDUCATION

Published by Creative Education
P.O. Box 227, Mankato, Minnesota 56002
Creative Education is an imprint of The Creative Company
www.thecreativecompany.us

Design and production by Blue Design
Art direction by Rita Marshall
Printed in the United States of America

Photographs by Corbis (Paul Benoit/AP, Bettmann, Steve
Lipofsky), Getty Images (Brian Babineau/NBAE, Steve
Babineau/NBAE, Andrew D. Bernstein/NBAE, Kevin C. Cox,
Tim DeFrisco, Steve Dunwell, Ron Hoskins/NBAE, Walter
Iooss Jr./NBAE, Walter Iooss Jr./Sports Illustrated, Manny
Millan/Sports Illustrated, NBAP/NBAE, Christian Petersen,
Dick Raphael/NBAE)

Library of Congress Cataloging-in-Publication Data
Whiting, Jim.
The story of the Boston Celtics / Jim Whiting.
p. cm. — (The NBA: a history of hoops)
Includes index.
Summary: An informative narration of the Boston Celtics
professional basketball team's history from its 1946
founding to today, spotlighting memorable players and
reliving dramatic events.
ISBN 978-1-60818-423-1
1. Boston Celtics (Basketball team)—History—Juvenile
literature. I. Title.

GV885.52.B67W56 2014
796.323'640974461—dc23   2013037440

CCSS: RI.5.1, 2, 3, 8; RH.6-8.4, 5, 7

First Edition
9 8 7 6 5 4 3 2 1

Cover: Guard Rajon Rondo
Page 2: Forward Tom Heinsohn (#15), center Bill Russell (#6)
Pages 4–5: Forward Paul Pierce
Page 6: Guard Dennis Johnson (#3), forward Larry Bird (#33)

TABLE OF CONTENTS

COURTSIDE STORIES

INTRODUCING...

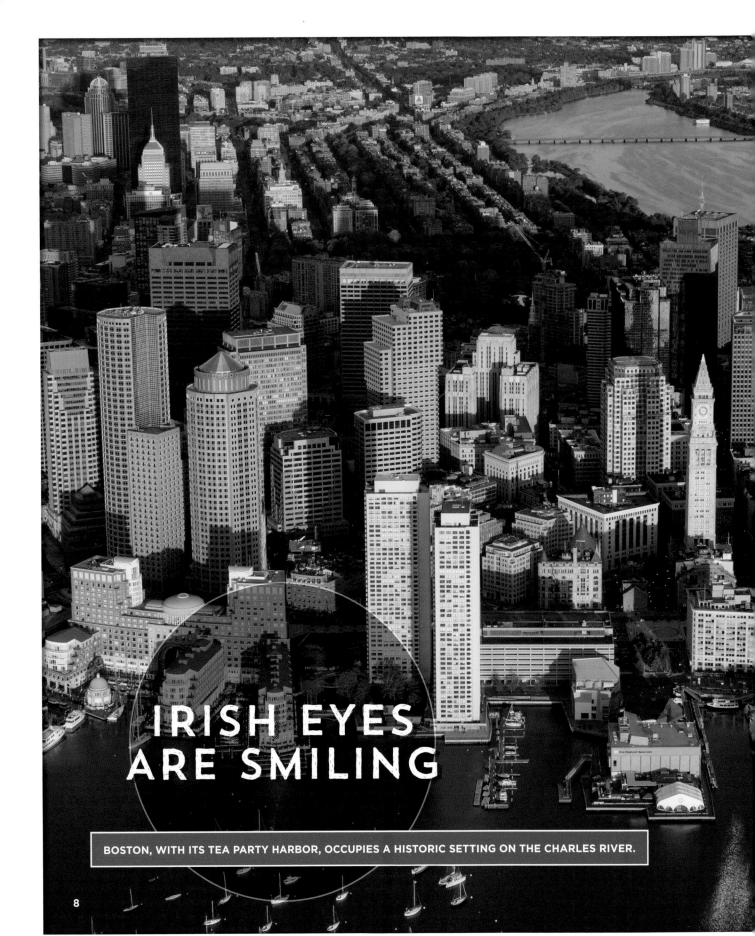

IRISH EYES ARE SMILING

BOSTON, WITH ITS TEA PARTY HARBOR, OCCUPIES A HISTORIC SETTING ON THE CHARLES RIVER.

Founded in 1630, the city of Boston, Massachusetts, became the focal point of resistance when the British began to impose strict taxes on the American colonies in the mid-1760s. Despite British attempts to punish them, Bostonians set an example of stubborn opposition that attracted followers throughout the colonies. Some of the city's leaders, such as John Hancock and John Adams, played key roles as the colonies declared their independence in 1776.

More than a century and a half later, Boston again took the lead in a national enterprise. With the end of World War II bringing military service members home, fans poured into sports arenas to watch professional hockey and college basketball again. But the owners of those arenas—such as Boston's Walter Brown—wanted something else to draw people into their buildings.

TEN YEARS AFTER THE CLUB'S FOUNDING, TOM HEINSOHN BROUGHT IT TO TITLE CONTENTION.

As *Philadelphia Inquirer* columnist Frank Fitzpatrick has explained, "At a New York meeting of the Arena Managers Association—operators of big-city arenas—several members supported ... Boston Garden owner Walter Brown, who wanted to form a pro basketball league." In 1946, Brown's plan became the 11-team Basketball Association of America (BAA). The new league set standards for the size of courts on which teams could play, the naming of teams according to home cities instead of corporate sponsors, and the rule that "no college boy will be signed up until his class

has graduated." The league also capped team payrolls at $40,000—less than what many of today's stars make in a single game.

For his new team, Brown considered names such as Unicorns, Whirlwinds, and Olympics before settling on the one that would become one of the most revered in all of professional sports: Celtics. "The name has a great tradition," Brown said. "And besides, Boston's full of Irishmen. We'll give them green uniforms and call them Celtics."

Brown had a limited knowledge of basketball, so he needed to hire an experienced head

COURTSIDE STORIES

THE FIRST CELTIC

Walter Brown (pictured seated, at center) took over as general manager of the Boston Garden after his father George, the arena's first general manager, passed away in 1937. In 1941, he was promoted to Garden president. Brown was so successful at promoting sports that he would go on to earn the title of "Boston's greatest sportsman," and according to sports historian Richard A. Johnson, it was well deserved: "[Brown] was simply a model of modesty, competence, and gentility in a profession filled with self-promotion, greed, and envy." Brown knew the unique nature of his enterprise. "You can't treat this like a straight business," he said. "It is too much of a business to be a sport and too much of a sport to be a business." Basketball wasn't his only contribution to the Boston sports scene. For nearly 25 years, he served as president of the Boston Athletic Association, the organization that produces the prestigious Boston Marathon. He also played a key role in pro and amateur hockey throughout New England. After he passed away in 1964, the Celtics organization retired jersey number 1 in his honor.

RED AUERBACH

Born in 1917, Red Auerbach began his coaching career in 1941 with a Washington, D.C.-area prep school and honed his skills with the U.S. Navy team during World War II. His first job at the professional level came in 1946 with the Washington Capitols of the BAA. Utilizing the new fast-break offense that Auerbach emphasized, the Capitols ran off a 17-game winning streak, a mark that wouldn't be exceeded for more than 20 years. After the fiery Auerbach clashed with the team owner two years later, he moved on to the Tri-Cities Blackhawks, only to conflict with management there as well. In Boston, though, he was a perfect fit. "I treated [players] with respect," he said. "I respected their intelligence. I was straight with them, and they were straight with me. I didn't lie to them, and they didn't lie to me. There was no double standard." Auerbach never left the organization, serving as team president until his death in 2006. Long before that, in 1985, the Celtics honored him by retiring jersey number 2, with his name on it.

"IF ONE OF HIS PLAYERS STEPPED OUT OF LINE, RED WOULD DESCEND ON HIM WITH BOTH FEET. YOU HAD TO RESPECT HIM, EVEN IF YOU DIDN'T LIKE HIM."

— BOB PETTIT ON RED AUERBACH

coach. He turned to John "Honey" Russell, who had molded Seton Hall University into a college powerhouse. In their first season, the Celtics had a 22–38 record, and that paltry win total seemed more a result of Irish luck than an abundance of talent. Although the Celtics boasted the league's fourth-best defense, their offense ranked dead last. Center Connie Simmons, who averaged 10.3 points per game, was the lone bright spot. The next season didn't get much better, though the Celtics achieved a playoff berth. They lost to the Chicago Stags in the first round.

After two disappointing seasons, Alvin "Doggie" Julian replaced Russell as coach. The switch made little impact. "Things were going so bad that even my wife wanted me to get out of the business," Brown said later. Despite his wife's protests, Brown spent most of their life savings to keep the struggling franchise out of bankruptcy. His tenacity and vision paid off. So did his decision to hire a brash young coach named Arnold "Red" Auerbach in 1950, a year after the BAA merged with the National Basketball League (NBL) to become the National Basketball Association (NBA).

Auerbach quickly established himself as an intimidating coach who would not tolerate losing. "If one of his players stepped out of line, Red would descend on him with both feet," former St. Louis Hawks forward Bob Pettit said. "You had to respect him, even if you didn't like him." Auerbach intimidated everyone in the arena—referees, fans, scorers, and opposing coaches—sometimes even physically. He also became infamous for lighting a cigar when a win was imminent.

Auerbach immediately laid the foundation for a championship team by acquiring point guard Bob Cousy in 1950 in the Chicago Stags dispersal draft and by trading for shooting guard Bill Sharman the following year. Cousy's sleight-of-hand passes sometimes fooled not only his opponents but his teammates as well. "Cousy was the catalyst for our team," said Auerbach. "He drove the guys to play their best." As the recipient of many of Cousy's passes, Sharman was widely regarded as being one of the best pure shooters to ever play in the NBA.

BOB COUSY

POSITION GUARD
HEIGHT 6-FOOT-1
CELTICS SEASONS
1950–63

When Bob Cousy was 13, he climbed a tree, slipped, crashed onto a sidewalk, and broke his right arm—his shooting arm. So he taught himself how to shoot and dribble left-handed and continued practicing. He was so dedicated that he promised himself that he would become a college All-American. He achieved that goal three times over at Massachusetts's College of the Holy Cross, but the nearby Celtics had no interest in him. "I'm supposed to win, not go after local yokels," responded coach Red Auerbach to protests when he didn't take Cousy in the 1950 NBA Draft. Cousy soon ended up playing for Auerbach, though—after the Celtics drew his name out of a hat in a dispersal draft when the Chicago Stags folded. He went on to astronomical heights as an NBA star. Cousy led the league in assists for 8 straight seasons, played in 13 consecutive All-Star Games, and won a Most Valuable Player (MVP) award. By then, Auerbach thought far more highly of the "local yokel." He proclaimed, "I've got news for you. There ain't nobody as good as Cooz. There never was."

BUILDING A DYNASTY

THE AGILE HEINSOHN WAS NICKNAMED "TOMMY GUN" FOR HIS RAPID-FIRE SHOOTING.

F rom 1950 to 1956, the Celtics made the playoffs every year but could never get past the division finals. Auerbach knew the kind of players he needed to win a championship, and he got them during the 1956 NBA Draft. He selected local Holy Cross forward Tom Heinsohn and University of San Francisco guard K. C. Jones. Then he orchestrated a draft-day trade for Jones's teammate, center Bill Russell.

Russell's league-leading rebounding average of 19.6 boards per game helped boost Boston to a 44–28 record. The Celtics went on to sweep the Syracuse Nationals in the Eastern Division finals and then met the Hawks in the NBA Finals. The deciding Game 7 was a classic, as the teams battled through two overtime periods before Boston finally pulled out a 125–123 victory to claim its first NBA championship. "Winning your first championship is always

INTRODUCING...

BILL
RUSSELL

POSITION CENTER
HEIGHT 6-FOOT-10
CELTICS SEASONS AS PLAYER
1956-69, AS PLAYER /
COACH 1966-69

Of all the amazing accomplishments Bill Russell achieved, perhaps his greatest was making defense a respectable part of the game. Red Auerbach had never seen Russell play in college, yet he traded for him in 1956 based on his reputation alone. Russell's aggressive style of play completely bewildered his opponents. He dished out punishment—with the help of his sharp elbows—as well as he absorbed it. He also used his intelligence to exploit the psychological aspects of the game, intimidating opponents by getting inside their heads. Russell figured if he could prevent a player from driving the lane, he had already won a major battle. He was so dominant that even he became aware of the whispers going around the league, joking in 1961, "They still call this club four shooters and Bill Russell." But nothing was farther from the truth. Russell was a team player who knew that the Celtics' success rested with all five players on the court working together. It was a philosophy he put into action to help Boston win 11 NBA titles (2 as player/coach).

the hardest," Auerbach said.

Little did the coach know that Boston's second attempt the following season would be even more difficult. In Game 3 of the 1958 Finals against St. Louis, Russell sprained his ankle. Although the ankle was taped and Russell gave a valiant effort in Game 6, the Hawks won the game by one point, 110–109, securing the championship as well. Cousy said, "Everyone knows how great Russell was and what he meant to us. He was severely hampered by that ankle. All I know is that without question, the Hawks were the second-best team that year."

he Celtics went on a rampage the following season and bombarded the Minneapolis Lakers in a four-game 1959 Finals sweep to take home their second title. Auerbach's continued preaching of fundamentals and emphasis on physical conditioning went a long way toward ensuring success. "By opening night, we were the best-conditioned team in the league," Sharman remembered. "Every year, he'd get us off to a great start, and that would bolster our confidence." The 1959–60 season was a prime example, as Boston began the season 30–4. Finishing with a 59–16 record, the team captured its third championship in four seasons.

With guard Sam Jones and forward Tom "Satch" Sanders adding extra punch, the Celtics racked up seven consecutive league championships from 1960 to 1966. Russell won the NBA's MVP award four times in that span, but in 1964, team owner Walter Brown passed away, and future Hall of Fame forward Frank Ramsey retired. Boston continued to roll along, clinching league titles again in 1965 and 1966.

In Game 7 of the 1965 Eastern Division finals, forward/guard John Havlicek made a memorable steal in the waning seconds to propel Boston past the Philadelphia 76ers and toward another title. In 1966, the Celtics followed the same road, beating the 76ers in the division finals and the Los Angeles Lakers in the NBA Finals. After winning his ninth title in a decade, Auerbach retired from coaching to become the team's general manager. Russell accepted the dual role of player/coach, thereby becoming the first African American coach in NBA history.

In Russell's first season, Boston lost the Eastern Division finals but bounced back in 1967–68 to win the first of two consecutive titles, bringing the franchise to a total of 11 in 13 years. "We felt we were good, we just didn't know how long we could keep it going," Havlicek later said. "We were just looking for one last gasp." And what a last gasp it was.

ROBERT PARISH

THE IMPORTANCE OF BEING BIG

Among the many innovative philosophies that Celtics coach Red Auerbach developed was the importance of obtaining dominant big men, and he proved its value time and again. The first such trade, in 1956, was considered a blockbuster. Auerbach sent two players (center Ed Macauley and forward Cliff Hagan) to the St. Louis Hawks for the Hawks' top draft pick, center Bill Russell (6-foot-10). That trade helped the Celtics develop into the most dominant franchise in NBA history. Then, in 1980, Auerbach dealt two high draft picks to the Golden State Warriors for veteran center Robert Parish (seven feet) and the third pick overall. Auerbach spun that pick into forward Kevin McHale (6-foot-10), thereby creating a stalwart frontcourt for the next decade. Finally, 27 years later, general manager Danny Ainge used the Auerbach principle to pry forward Kevin Garnett (6-foot-11) away from the Minnesota Timberwolves, courtesy of Minnesota's team president, Kevin McHale. The very next season, the Celtics won the franchise's 17th championship. Like Russell, Parish, and McHale, Garnett proved once again that talented big men lead to titles.

DOWN AND UP AGAIN

JO JO WHITE (#10) SET A CELTICS RECORD FOR CONSECUTIVE GAMES PLAYED (488).

W hen Russell retired in 1969, it seemed the Celtics' magic went with him. Though new coach Tom Heinsohn inherited a lineup that featured veterans such as forwards Don Nelson and Larry Siegfried, the team went just 34–48. It was Boston's first losing record in 20 years.

By 1970, many experts thought the Celtics were in for a long rebuilding period. But those experts underestimated Auerbach's managerial skills. He installed versatile rookie Dave Cowens at center, moved Havlicek up front with the improving Nelson, and revamped the backcourt with young guards Don Chaney and Jo Jo White. Havlicek starred in his best offensive season ever, netting a career-high 28.9 points per game to become the league's second-best scorer. By the time the 1971–72 campaign

DAVE COWENS

COURTSIDE STORIES

THE FABULOUS FIFTH

In 1976, Boston met the Phoenix Suns in an NBA Finals series highlighted by a Game 5 that is known as the "Fabulous Fifth"—one of only two NBA Finals games ever to go into triple overtime. In the waning seconds of the first overtime, Phoenix forward Curtis Perry drained four straight points to force a second overtime. With five seconds remaining in the second overtime, Perry dropped another bucket to give the Suns a 110–109 edge. Then Boston forward John Havlicek hit the apparent game-winning shot. But referee Richie Powers signaled that there was one second left to play. So Suns coach John MacLeod tried to get creative and called a timeout—one that Phoenix didn't have. While that infraction gave Boston guard Jo Jo White one technical foul shot and the Celtics a two-point edge, it also allowed Phoenix a final inbound pass to forward Gar Heard, who hit a miraculous shot from near midcourt to force the third overtime. That's when Celtics backup center Jim Ard became the unlikely hero, contributing eight points in the 128–126 victory. Two days later, Boston captured its lucky 13th NBA championship.

began, the Celtics were potent contenders again behind the emerging stardom of Cowens. The prized left-handed shooter became the league's premier pivot man as well as Boston's undisputed floor leader.

The following season, Boston soared to a franchise-record 68 victories, and Cowens earned league MVP honors. "We play Celtics basketball," explained Havlicek. "We work hard every night, and we don't care who gets the glory. It's all about the team." As if to prove Havlicek's point, one of the season's unforeseen bright spots was the rebounding prowess of forward Paul Silas, who had been obtained from the Phoenix Suns in a trade. Unfortunately, the Celtics' sterling regular season gave way to postseason disappointment. For the second straight year, Boston lost the Eastern

CELTICS TEAMS OF THE EARLY AND MID-1970s WORKED TOGETHER TO COVER THE COURT.

JOHN HAVLICEK

POSITION FORWARD / GUARD
HEIGHT 6-FOOT-5
CELTICS SEASONS
1962–78

When John "Hondo" Havlicek entered the league in 1962, he was known as a defensive specialist for the 1960 college national champion Ohio State Buckeyes. "I realized that the most difficult player to guard is the kind of player who is always moving," Havlicek said. So once Hondo hit the court, he never stopped. "You just wind him up—click, click, click—he keeps going," laughed center Bill Russell. Teammate Bob Cousy wasn't convinced and figured Havlicek for just another "nonshooter who would probably burn himself out." But Havlicek, who played both forward and guard, proved the doubters wrong and became one of the most dangerous two-way players in league history. Hondo led Boston in scoring 10 times and in assists 6 times and was the team's captain for more than a decade. But his proudest moment came on November 20, 1976, when he played his 1,123rd pro game—more than anyone else had ever played at the time. "If there's any phase of basketball I've been identified with, it's endurance," he later said. "When I broke the old record, it meant a great deal to me."

"WE PLAY CELTICS BASKETBALL. WE WORK HARD EVERY NIGHT, AND WE DON'T CARE WHO GETS THE GLORY. IT'S ALL ABOUT THE TEAM."

— JOHN HAVLICEK ON TEAMWORK

Conference finals to the New York Knicks.

Coach Heinsohn finally got an NBA championship the next season against the Milwaukee Bucks, but it didn't come easily. After the teams traded victories through the first five Finals contests, center Kareem Abdul-Jabbar and guard Oscar Robertson helped Milwaukee scramble to a 102–101 double-overtime win in Game 6. But in the finale, Cowens out-dueled them and led Boston to a 102–87 victory, bringing its championship count to a full dozen.

lthough they amassed 60 wins in 1974–75, the Celtics were outmatched in the conference finals against the Washington Bullets. However, the 1975–76 Celtics rose to championship heights once more, winning a thrilling NBA Finals series over Phoenix. The 35-year-old Havlicek, though hobbled by a leg injury, led Boston to victories in the first two games. After the Celtics dropped the next two, they also nearly lost Game 5 at home. But they hung on during three overtime periods to outlast Phoenix 128–126. The anticlimactic Game 6 was a cakewalk

in comparison, as Boston claimed its 13th championship trophy.

Just as the Celtics stumbled at the end of the 1960s with the retirements of Auerbach and Russell, they also faltered as the '70s concluded, this time due to the retirements of Coach Heinsohn and Havlicek. Heinsohn had carved out a new spot for himself in Celtics history. One of the club's most successful but underrated players in the 1950s and '60s, he had turned into a coaching mastermind. His 427 victories were the second-most in club history. Tom Sanders, Heinsohn's successor, could not fill such massive shoes, and the Celtics descended to the league's lower rungs.

FORWARD MARVIN BARNES
(#27) AND GUARD CHRIS
FORD COULDN'T DEFEND
AGAINST A 29–53 TEAM
RECORD IN 1979.

BIRD IN THE
CELTICS NEST

CEDRIC MAXWELL HELPED BOSTON ELBOW ITS WAY TO CHAMPIONSHIPS IN THE 1980s.

Auerbach needed to find new talent. In 1977, he chose forward Cedric "Cornbread" Maxwell in the NBA Draft, and in 1978, he traded for point guard Nate "Tiny" Archibald. Also in 1978, Auerbach drafted forward Larry Bird from Indiana State University. Bird joined the team a year later, just after Boston had suffered its worst 2-year stretch ever—winning just 61 games combined in 1977–78 and 1978–79. Bird's savvy play helped the Celtics match that win total in just one marvelous resurrection season. New coach Bill Fitch won the NBA Coach of the Year award, and Bird earned Rookie of the Year honors en route to one of the greatest careers in the NBA.

In 1980, Auerbach brought in workhorse center Robert "Chief" Parish from the Golden State Warriors and spent a first-round draft pick on University of Minnesota forward

PLAYING CHECKERS

The most famous floor in NBA history was built of scrap hardwood from Tennessee in the Boston Arena (where the team played some home games) for its inaugural season in 1946, and then it was moved to the Boston Garden in 1952. To get the most out of the recycled material, the 247 panels—each measuring 5' x 5' square and 1.5" thick—were laid in an alternating pattern to achieve the floor's distinctive checkerboard appearance. The floor was not uniform in its resiliency, and Boston players knew just where the dead spots were located. They often prodded opposing dribblers to those very same dead spots to take advantage of odd bounces and steal the ball. "The parquet floor is synonymous with the Celtics," said Red Auerbach. "If teams felt it was a poor floor, I used it for an advantage by playing with their minds." When the team moved to the Fleet Center (now known as TD Garden) in 1995, the floor went with it. Four years later, it finally went into honorable retirement. Most of it was cut up and sold as souvenirs, though a few pieces were worked into a new floor—which retains the checkerboard look.

Kevin McHale. The reloaded Celtics barreled to a 62–20 mark and stormed to the NBA Finals, where "The Big Three" of Bird, Parish, and McHale overwhelmed the scrappy Houston Rockets in six games.

fter Boston was eliminated in the early rounds of the playoffs the next two years, former guard K. C. Jones was hired as head coach. He boosted the 1983–84 Celtics back to the NBA Finals, where they faced superstar guard Magic Johnson and the Lakers. Boston lost Game 1 and was on the verge of losing Game 2 when guard Gerald Henderson intercepted a crosscourt pass and tied the game with an easy layup. The Celtics went on to win that contest but lost the next. After pushing Game 4 into overtime, Boston took 2 of the final 3 games for its 15th championship.

The Big Three did not make up the whole show in Boston, especially during the team's glowing 1985–86 season. Guard Dennis Johnson brought a championship-caliber competitive attitude to the table, having been a member of the victorious 1979 Seattle SuperSonics. Guard

Danny Ainge provided a spark with his steady ball-handling, and veteran center Bill Walton helped hold the team together.

The 1985–86 Celtics lost only one game at home and were expected to go the distance. But the Celtics had to get past their old coach Bill Fitch and his Houston Rockets, which included the "Twin Towers" of forward Ralph Sampson and center Hakeem Olajuwon. Fitch could tell that this Celtics crew was stronger than the one he had coached. "More important than the talent," he marveled, "they were totally devoid of any players who thought personal statistics meant anything." Yet individuals such as Bird stood out. "Larry Legend" dominated Game 6, recording a triple-double (double-digit tallies in 3 categories) with 29 points, 11 rebounds, and 12 assists to help claim Boston's 16th NBA championship.

Although Boston reached the Finals the next season, the Lakers won the series four games to two. Then, as with Boston's previous dynasties, the Big Three era endured a late-decade slump, spurred in part by successive tragedies. In 1986, the Celtics drafted University of Maryland forward Len Bias, expected to become the team's next star. Tragically, he died two days

LARRY BIRD

POSITION FORWARD
HEIGHT 6-FOOT-9
CELTICS SEASONS
1979–92

When Indiana State University basketball coach Bob King found Larry Bird, the former high school star was driving a garbage truck in his hometown of French Lick, Indiana. Bird had left rival Indiana University in 1974, during his first season, and King could tell that Bird still longed to play. So he convinced Bird to try again at Indiana State. Bird obliged, and in his senior year, he took the Sycamores to the 1979 college national championship game, where they lost to Magic Johnson's Michigan State University Spartans. Bird wasn't particularly gifted physically, but he practiced constantly. "I always know what's happening on the court," he said. "I know exactly what I can and cannot do." The three-time NBA MVP with the sweet shooting stroke also had nerves of steel, especially in the clutch. As the guest of honor the night the Celtics paid tribute to Bird, longtime rival Magic Johnson said, "I always told people that Larry Bird was the best all-around player that ever played the game. But more than that, he was the one player I feared and respected more than anyone else."

later. The next year, Boston drafted Reggie Lewis, a multitalented forward. Lewis became the team's leader when Bird was forced to retire in 1992 because of chronic back problems. Bird finished his Hall of Fame career with averages of 24.3 points, 10 rebounds, and 6.3 assists. Sadly, Lewis's tenure as Bird's replacement was short-lived, as he died suddenly of a heart attack in July 1993.

After the shocking deaths of Bias and Lewis, the Celtics suffered several losing seasons in the 1990s. Looking to rebuild after moving into the new Fleet Center arena in 1995, Boston hired successful college coach Rick Pitino in 1997. But Pitino would never take the Celtics to a winning record. Young players such as forwards Antoine Walker and Paul Pierce showed flashes of brilliance but struggled while adjusting to the pro game. In 2001, Jim O'Brien replaced Pitino and coached the Celtics to their first winning season (49–33) in nearly a decade.

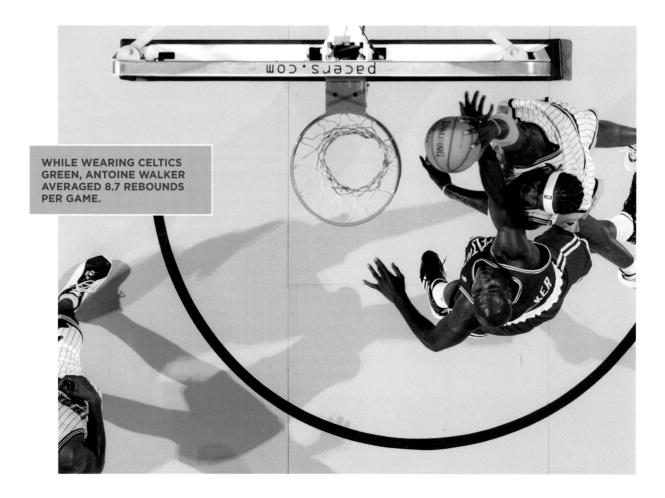

WHILE WEARING CELTICS GREEN, ANTOINE WALKER AVERAGED 8.7 REBOUNDS PER GAME.

COURTSIDE STORIES
TWIN TRAGEDIES

June 1986 should have been another magical month in Celtics history. On June 8, the team won its 16th NBA championship. Nine days later in the NBA Draft, Red Auerbach engineered a trade to land University of Maryland forward Len Bias, perhaps the most talented collegiate player available, with the second overall pick. However, June 19 seemed to be the day that the "Celtic Mystique" ran out when Bias died of a drug overdose. "It hurt our sport," said famous Duke University coach Mike Krzyzewski. "Above and beyond the loss of life, we never got to see one of those truly great ones become great." In an effort to move past the Bias tragedy, the Celtics selected Reggie Lewis from nearby Northeastern University in the next year's draft. Lewis lived up to his potential, becoming the team's captain and an All-Star. But in July 1993, during an off-season shootaround, Lewis collapsed and died of a heart attack. These twin tragedies had lasting negative repercussions on the Celtics franchise for many years afterward.

37

RETURNING TO GREATNESS

KEVIN GARNETT RENEWED THE CELTICS' ENTHUSIASM WHEN HE ARRIVED IN 2007.

Pierce and Walker each averaged 20 or more points per game for 3 straight seasons from 2000–01 through 2002–03. The talented duo, along with point guard Kenny Anderson, brought the Celtics to the 2002 Eastern Conference finals, where they were outmatched by Anderson's former team, the upstart New Jersey Nets. Things got worse the next season when Boston was swept by the same Nets team in the second round of the playoffs.

Just before the 2003–04 season, Boston traded Walker to the Dallas Mavericks. Even without a steady partner, Pierce showed his pedigree by carrying the Celtics to the 2004 playoffs, where they were swept by the Indiana Pacers in the first round. In 2004–05, under new coach Doc Rivers, the Celtics were noticeably stronger and proved it by winning the Atlantic Division—their first division title

since 1992. But once again, they lost to Indiana in the postseason.

Boston had found relatively little success in the 21 years since it had won its 16th title. After back-to-back losing seasons in 2005–06 and 2006–07—the latter included a franchise-record 18-game losing streak—the Celtics traded for All-Star shooting guard Ray Allen. The Celtics then pulled off a historic swap, trading five players and two draft picks to acquire Minnesota Timberwolves star forward Kevin Garnett. Once again, references to "The Big Three" were being thrown around Boston—this time meaning Pierce, Garnett, and Allen. "Winning a championship," said Danny Ainge, who had become Boston's executive director of basketball operations in 2003, "is now a legitimate and realistic goal."

Bolstered by talent on all sides, including youthful spark plugs such as guard Rajon Rondo and center Kendrick Perkins, the Celtics made history again by orchestrating the NBA's greatest one-year turnaround, transforming from a 24–58 disgrace in 2007–08 into a 66–16 juggernaut. En route to Boston's defeating the Lakers for its 17th NBA championship, Garnett became the first Celtics player ever to capture the NBA's Defensive Player of the Year award.

After the Celtics were bounced from the second round of the 2009 playoffs, many experts thought the team's veteran stars were finally washed up. But in 2009–10, Boston surged back to the NBA Finals and very nearly captured its 18th title. As Rondo emerged as a true star, the Celtics took

PAUL PIERCE

POSITION FORWARD
HEIGHT 6-FOOT-6
CELTICS SEASONS
1998–2013

Paul Pierce left the University of Kansas in 1998 after earning the Big 12 Conference's tournament MVP honors in both his sophomore and junior years. He kept the momentum going in Boston with a tremendous rookie season, highlighted by starting 47 games, being Boston's top scorer 16 times, and becoming a player around whom the team could build. His reputation as a clutch performer who elevated his game against the NBA's top competition spread beyond the Eastern Conference. That notoriety led Los Angeles Lakers star center Shaquille O'Neal to bestow on Pierce the nickname "The Truth." What started as just a flattering moniker soon turned into an opportunity, as Pierce started The Truth Fund in 2002 to provide educational opportunities for youth. Since then, he has established The Truth on Health Campaign and the Paul Pierce Center for Minimally Invasive Surgery at Tufts Medical Center and Floating Hospital for Children. He has also hosted hundreds of families for Thanksgiving and Christmas dinners. In 2013, he even made himself available as a prize in the Massachusetts Lottery Boston Celtics Sweepstakes. The winner got to play a game of H-O-R-S-E with Pierce.

AS OF 2014, RAJON RONDO HAD APPEARED IN THREE NBA FINALS SERIES WITH BOSTON.

RAY ALLEN

WHEN IN ROME, "UBUNTU!"

"Ubuntu!" The Celtics shouted after every practice during the 2007–08 championship season. Coach Doc Rivers said he chose the chant after reading about South African leader Desmond Tutu that summer. "Ubuntu," a word from the African Bantu language, stresses collective success over individual achievement. The chant had an effect on the players, especially newly arrived superstars Kevin Garnett and Ray Allen, who went out of their way to make sure every player knew the team could succeed only if they played as a unit. During the team's preseason exhibition trip to Rome, Italy, Paul Pierce, Rajon Rondo, and Kendrick Perkins shaved their heads to honor their new bald-headed teammates. The players often hung out together while abroad, and Garnett and Pierce even organized a team outing to watch a soccer game. "Those guys are stars, and they could have easily taken their own limos," rookie guard Gabe Pruitt said. "But they rode over with the rest of us in a bus." The team was coming together in the Red Auerbach tradition. Eight months after bonding in Rome, that Celtics crew became NBA champions.

a three-games-to-two lead over the rival Lakers in the Finals, only to lose the final two contests in Los Angeles. "I told our guys after the game I couldn't have been prouder of this group," Coach Rivers said after his team lost 83–79 in Game 7. "We're not going to be the same team next year. Guys are not going to be there, so that was tough for me. But I was just proud."

he team may not have been the same in 2010–11, but the results were similar. The Celtics went 56–26 and swept New York in the first round of the playoffs. But they ran into an energized Miami Heat squad in the conference semifinals, losing four games to one.

In the strike-shortened 2011–12 season, the Celtics won the Atlantic Division for the fifth straight season. After tough series wins over the Atlanta Hawks and the 76ers in the first two playoff rounds, the Celtics faced Miami in the conference finals. With the series tied 3–3, Boston opened up an 11-point second-quarter lead in the final game. The Celtics couldn't hold on to it, though, and lost 101–88.

The 2012 NBA Draft brought Ohio State power forward Jared Sullinger to bolster the Celtics' front-court depth. With Allen's free-agent departure for the Miami Heat, the Celtics acquired veteran guards Jason Terry and Courtney Lee to replace him. "We are very excited that we were able to acquire Courtney Lee," said Ainge. "Courtney brings a vast set of tools on both ends of the court and will be a great fit on our roster."

Lee needed to be a "great fit." The Celtics had perhaps the worst-ever injury week in NBA history during the 2012–13 season, losing both Rondo and Sullinger (who by then was a starter) over a five-day span beginning in late January. Lee and other role-players had to fill the sudden void. "We have to be a team by committee," Coach Rivers said (during what would be his last full season in Boston). "I'm asking guys to play different spots." The "committee" responded with a seven-game winning streak after Rondo went down but couldn't sustain the momentum, ending 41–40. Boston then lost to the Knicks in the first round of the playoffs, four games to two. Within days after the season's end, speculation about the team's future—especially regarding Pierce and Garnett—began. Both stars were traded to the Brooklyn Nets in June 2013, and in 2014, the Celtics looked to players such as newly appointed team captain Rondo to become more consistent contributors to the team.

Little did Walter Brown realize that the team he organized nearly seven decades ago to fill up his arena would become one of the league's premier franchises. Boston's tally of 17 championships is 1 ahead of the Lakers' and stakes the claim to the most-ever NBA titles. The Celtics trail only the Lakers in total number of regular-season games won and number of playoff appearances. Many of the men who donned Celtics green—such as Bob Cousy, Bill Russell, and Larry Bird—are among the league's all-time greats. And even in an era of increasing parity—when 6 different teams have been NBA champions in the past 10 years—the Boston Celtics almost certainly will remain among the league's elite for years to come.

INDEX